LITTLE DEATHS

Shilo Niziolek

Riot in Your Throat
publishing fierce, feminist poetry

Niziolek, Shilo
1st edition.
ISBN: 979-8-9889898-2-0

Cover Art: Rachel Mulder
Cover Design: Kirsten Birst
Book Design: Shanna Compton
Author Photo: Shilo Niziolek

Riot in Your Throat
Arlington, VA
www.riotinyourthroat.com

For my sister, Brittany, who isn't a big poetry person, but who always reads mine, who shows up, whether it be for a board game night, a gossip sesh, or on the day my dog dies. I wish we were still in our bunk beds, giggling late into the night.

"And when everything else is gone, you can be rich in loss."
—Rebecca Solnit, *A Field Guide to Getting Lost*

CONTENTS

WHEN ████████████████████████████

████████████████████████████ you

offer ████████████████████████

ghost stories ████████████████████

████ the almost dying, ████████████ die

████████████████████████████████

████████ Everyone ████████████ turning

████████████████████████████████

████████████ you,

into a bear trundling ████████████, a frog

crossing ████████████████████████

a weasel ████████████████████ snapping the neck.

Again ████████████████████████████

████████████████ your own decay ████████

████████████████████████████████████

blackberry brambles ████████████████████████

████████████ the same stretch of highway ████████████

████████████████████████████████████

████████████████████████████

████████████████████████████████

where the road splits.

WHEN TRAUMA WON'T RELEASE ITS GRIP

Sometimes, the things that happen to you
offer no room for escape. You want to write
ghost stories but you just make the same
loops on the paper: domestic abuse, chronic
illness, the almost dying, watching the dog die
in the same spot on the grass, sunshiney day
after day. Everyone around you turning
pain into hieroglyphs, chicken scratch on
dirt floor, but you, you can't turn your pain
into a bear trundling through woods, a frog
crossing a lonely cavernous road in the fog,
a weasel sneaking into the coop and snapping the neck.

Again and again you tread the same circles, trudge
through the mud of your own decay, prick your
finger, your arm, your hair getting caught in
blackberry brambles—every September coming up red.
You're on the same stretch of highway where he left you
after tossing your keys into the thorns. You'll never get
off the highway, cars rushing past and no one
stopping. You'll never see what's around the bend
where the road splits.

THAT'S WHAT THE WATER GAVE ME
—after Florence & The Machine

At the pool, no one speaks to me.
I place little red balls of wax, formed

by my smooth fingers
I float on my back to the sound of bodies

moving through water. Each, their own
tidal wave of small griefs, come to the water:

is it to forget the body or to become only body—
finned, buoyant—some of the older ladies in their

body suits bob up and down the lanes, moonwalking
across the surface of the universe, like aged gods, what

triumph in their gaits, out of the pool they hobble,
grab for canes left in the open air, use the rails

to usher their bodies, afterward, into the heat of
the tub. I see the way they look at me: mid-30s

covered in tattoos, fully-fucking-alive, they must
think, but imagine me here, under water, drowning

out the sounds of humans, of my grief. It circles—
shark-infested, rapturous, electric-eeled under the

hush of anxiety, of illness, of watching the world burn,
and me inside it, me, missing a dog so desperately,

telling my partner, *no, I'm sorry, no, no, no,* until

I'm out of breath, out of body, gasping to come propelling out,
to turn up on another coast in a different body,

something altogether more forgiving than this one.
The water laps my body, and I, frog-legged,

lap the pool, slowly, slower still than some of these
elders, their hands cut like blades through the surface.

I am underneath, under the water, goggles pressed tightly,
I marvel at their bodies, all grace, all survival, all tsunamied.

At the edge, we hoist our bodies from the wake, we fill
our lungs, we do not lay on our sides, flapping on the shore.

TRIPTYCH FROM A BOX OF DARKNESS

—after Mary Oliver

I.

Someone I once loved used to say to me, *I made you. You were nothing, knew nothing before me.* As if destruction is the same thing as creation. He thought he was the before and the after, I, a mere canvas for his want.

II.

But didn't I come, first and always, from my mother and her mother and her mother and hers? Wasn't it the fields they tilled, hands dug deep in the soil, wasn't it the knit, stitch, pearl of yarn in their hands, and aren't I part scale from the fish they filleted, part bark from the peel of the axes they swung, puffs of flour from dough they pounded with their own two hands? Wasn't I, first and foremost, from the rocking chair, my mom's body swaying below me, her voice a quiet ushering force in the dark, the pat of her hand lulling me to sleep?

III.

And after all the mothers and the mothers' mothers, there was the Shoshone River, Beck Lake, miles and miles of Wyoming desert, cattails in the wind, girls who placed their heads close together to link up dreams of horses as they slept, a sister and her Backstreet Boys, NSYNC, Britney Spears, Christina Aguilera posters lining our shared wall, a brother who I read a story to the day he wanted to run away after the memory of a recalled memory—my mother telling me how at two I packed a bag to run away and then stood on the sidewalk bawling until she read me a story—all the years and years and years of her stories, the ghosts most of all, and the young boys who played me Metallica long before he entered the scene, and after, after myself, unmothered and untethered from the *you*, there was a warm home, a quiet love, and my hands in the soil, pulling up grass and planting down lavender, oregano, thyme, and a rosemary bush now grown to my waist. Small births and the dogs that surround me, the country music of my ancestors on the radio, and the sound of the keys on my laptop clattering with the grading of papers, editing of books, pounding of poems, I, fully myself which is to say parts of the many, parts of the whole, not one act of unforgiveness to complete me.

WHEN WE ██ LEARN ██████

our heart ██
We cry ██
██████

We cry ██
████████
██████ muted,
██████
circling ██████
██████
████████
██████████
██████

We cry with our bodies
████████
██████
██████ barking,
██ licking, shredding
██ bouncing, ██ bathing.

████████
playing ██ every night,
██████
██████ tumbling

across the ▮▮▮ *Risk* ▮
▮▮ rolling ▮
▮ while ▮▮
▮▮
▮▮
▮ sneaking ▮
▮ exposed
by ▮

▮
▮ love, so much of it,
▮ all along.

WHEN WE FIRST LEARN SHE'S DYING

Our piggy, pig-snout,
snouter-faust,
snout-un-dane-tangler,
misses snooty,
huff-and-puffer,
our heart dog, we cry.
We cry on the way
to the emergency room.

We cry in the lobby,
a documentary about meerkats
on the television muted,
filling out the clipboard,
circling *do not resuscitate*,
if it comes to that,
in the room when they say
tumor, abdomen, slow-bleed, rupture,
eventuality, chances.

We cry with our bodies
curled around her, small paw
in large human hands.
But then she begins barking,
begins licking, shredding
toys, bouncing, sunbathing.

In the evenings, we begin
playing Farkle. Not every night,
but more than before.
The sound of 6 dice tumbling

across the coffee table. *Risk it all*,
he says, over and over, rolling his last
die, while she curls up on the floor
beside me, or drapes herself over
my knees, or sits on the couch
behind me, sneaking licks
of my neck skin, exposed
by my short hair.

Risk it all, he says,
like this love, so much of it,
isn't what we've been doing all along.

ELEGY TAXONOMY

How they awaited him, those little deaths!
They waited like sweethearts.
                  —Sylvia Plath, "The Rabbit Catcher"

There were the little deaths.
Meaning the ways in which we lose
things: keys, a favorite hoodie, then
those other *little* things, drifting
away on time's tide:

a friend, another friend,
someone we loved, another
someone, someones-on-someones,
calls we no longer make to relationships
broken. Soon we are body-lined,
we make little shrines to
the little deads.

Then, the big deaths.

My grandma, the memory
of her rubbing sleep from my fingers at 4 a.m.
And now when my feet sleep, go numb,
after a three-year ache, the exams
coming—nerve conduction, spinal
x-ray, brain MRI—more

little deaths, and the yearn
for her to be alive, for me to stumble
out to her, let her
absorb the tingling.

Then there were animals: the cat
whose kidneys shut down,
my older sister and I crouching above
his limp body, tiny mewls as he
laid on gravel, sharp final resting.
Then dogs, then cats again, deer hanging
from garage rafters.

And the dogs coming soon
that terrible future I can't contend
with; these things all placed out of
order, the sweethearts, little big deaths.

Then, before we watched tallies
soar from an airborne
annihilator, there was planes
hitting buildings. After, but before
tallies, there was my middle school
boyfriend and the dream where he
visited, kissed me lightly looking
like the 15-year-old I knew,
telling me it would be okay,
laughing on his way out
of the scene, forever 27.

Before and after there were
overdoses of people I used
to know. And during the tallies
there was the pine siskin squatted
below my feeder, unable to eat, ushered
into a box predeath, how unpoetic
of me, my gloved hands.

There were fast-growing
lesions scraped from my womb
and the document I signed beforehand,
there was the clotted knot of hardened
blood in the rivers of my legs.
But before that there was,
suctioned up with a tube in
a triage unit, past the swinging
white double doors, the deceleration
of my heart, and the ruby red
slippers for the child that would
never come, never put them on
feet and tap *home, home, home.*

Now here's me, the little little deaths
like *Stuart Little*, like *The Borrowers*,
their tiny teapots making tiny
homes in me, moss-coated,
deer-stricken, spike-hearted.

WYOMING CONJURE

I hear my mom calling,
flung open the front door
of our double-wide.

We're out making
molehills into mountains,
towers, forests, cities.

Our hands thick with mud.

And if we guessed,
we'd never guess.
We can't go home.

The succulents never
sit plump at our knees.
Dogs will never bark the same.

I'll watch the image of my mom
toss wildflower seeds
in the flower box out front.

Hands like mine.

Follow her shape
follow the rectangle of the yard
green garden hose spouting well water
that we turn into frog ponds.

I won't climb the dumpster
to survey my world.
And the neighbor won't come and complain.

The dogs and cats have died,
the moon too.

No desert tongues.
No Wyoming howl.

I only think of what is lost
in the bright light of 6 a.m.

The coyotes only sing when I ask them to.

ON AGING

I want to write a little
poem. Like a tiny sliver
of my mom's blackberry
cheesecake. Sweet and tart,
pulled right from the brambles
behind her house. But then the urge
to extend, string it out, keep my mom
in the kitchen, pressing fingers into pie
crusts until the end of time. But there she
is at the red-framed window, hand flying to
her mouth as she glances up in time to see her
favorite chicken, Salt and Pepper, always flitting
over the coop to peck at the delicacies in the garden,
swooped up broad daylight, blur of red fur as the fox slinks back into the woods.

WHEN THE AIR ▉▉▉▉▉ **BREAKS**
▉▉▉▉▉

We were ▉▉▉▉▉
▉▉▉▉▉
▉▉▉▉▉ house
▉ our boards ▉ metaphorical,
▉ we were ▉▉▉▉▉
outside ▉▉▉▉▉

▉▉▉▉▉
▉▉▉▉▉
▉▉▉▉▉
▉▉▉
▉▉▉▉▉
▉▉▉
the strike of ▉▉▉▉▉

▉ smoke,
▉▉▉▉▉
▉▉▉▉
▉▉▉▉
the dry dead grass,
▉▉▉▉▉

▉▉▉▉▉
your lungs ▉▉▉ quicksand
▉▉▉▉ a thousand ▉
▉ bites and ▉▉▉
▉▉▉▉▉

All across ▉▉▉▉
▉▉▉▉ foggy orange skies,

a  hellscape
blood red

We slept
asphyxiated,
our

head underwater

bleary-eyed,

I was

hammered down
untethered

gathered artifacts

mildly hazardous

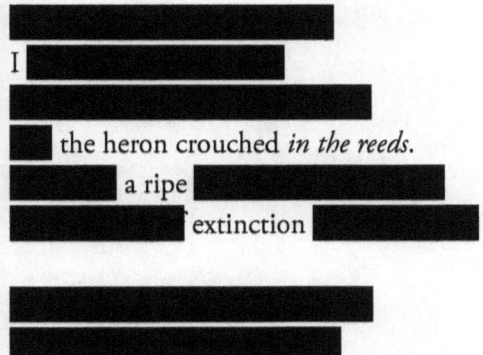

I ▮▮▮▮▮▮▮▮▮▮▮

▮ the heron crouched *in the reeds*.
▮ a ripe
▮ extinction ▮▮▮

WHEN THE AIR QUALITY INDEX BREAKS

Oregon, September 2020

We were boarded up in her homes
in the bad part of town.
We weren't a meth house
and our boards were metaphorical,
but we were isolated against the plague
outside our windows nonetheless.

I stopped working and
he worked outside all day,
his neck turned leather
from the sun
when the forest lit up,
all around the city,
the strike of innumerable matches.

The smoke,
it littered the world,
the windshields,
the lawn chairs,
the dry dead grass,
everywhere a layer of ash.

When you stepped outside
your lungs filled with quicksand
and your eyes a thousand tiny
ant bites and your heart
slowed to a dangerous pace.

All across the internet
pictures of foggy orange skies,

a delivery truck with the hellscape
background of blood red air.

We slept the sleep of the dead,
the sleep of the asphyxiated,
our hands held tightly around
our own necks.

Can you imagine holding
your own head underwater
until you drowned?
Because that's what we were doing,
have been doing all along.

And when I woke, bleary-eyed,
frog-hearted, like an ash winter
had fallen over us and I was
hibernating to preserve until spring.

We did it then, hammered down
the boarded-up windows, untethered
shackles, for only Snow White can
sleep for fourteen plus hours and not be dead.

We gathered artifacts: Ziploc bags
of pictures, birth certificates,
a favorite hoodie and our dogs.
We drove to the coast where the air
was only mildly hazardous,
salted clean.

In the wee hours of morning
I walked to the marshes.
A cool mist hung over the water
and the heron crouched *in the reeds*.
I plucked a ripe September blackberry,
felt the burst of extinction on my tongue.

We hunkered low, waited it out,
held our breath, still holding.

PEOPLE SAY THEY HATE SMALL TALK & DON'T WANT TO TALK ABOUT THE WEATHER

But my best friend, the one
I tell my deepest secrets to,
who once asked me, early in
our friendship, what it was like
to leave someone you still loved,
to pretend they don't exist, and
who listened, long legs curled up
beside her, feet in mismatched socks
crossed at the ankle, as I told her
you can't always be with someone
you love because either you leave them
and turn them into a ghost, or you
stay and allow yourself to become
one instead, is the same friend who
weekly sends me updates about the weather,
two hours' drive down snaking rivers
separating us, land masses and micro
climates, and I update her on the same.
Sometimes, the only way to say *I miss
you* is: the wind is kicking up and
there's a rainstorm on the way.

I'M NOT SUPPOSED TO BE WRITING POEMS ABOUT YOU ANYMORE.

That's what I told myself. But
last night you appeared in the room
of an old friend's house. We went
outside to smoke, as if I hadn't given up
cigarettes and loving you a decade ago,
and I said, *I'm still in love with you,*
and you said, *all the girls are,* like I
was one in a long string of first
loves that will never get over you.
Later, walking down a dark street,
there you were, cast in the streetlight, you
and your hands on me.
I woke ragged with desire.

MARY OLIVER SAID I DON'T HAVE TO BE GOOD

Outside the cherry tomatoes fall
off the vine, rot in the yard.

I move the pot toward the birdbath
where the crows might find them.

Inside, I pretend to not know
what I know about the way things

are crumbling, steady and at a
quickening pace. All around us

extinction, disaster after disaster
after disaster with no release,

fanatics trying to wipe out our words,
our bodies, our power.

Outside, I walk to the early
autumn tree, bright orange like a flame

to the sky, just to see it up close
after driving by, just to stand

under its branches and look up.
Inside, I still dream about a body

I haven't touched in nearly fifteen years.
His body over my body, in a crowd,

in the woods, on an empty street,
everywhere I turn, there he is,

a curse, a spell, a wish.
I get down on my knees. I turn.

Outside, there's still smoke
in the air, despite the rains we've been getting.

If you listen close enough,
quiet your heart, tune your ears,

you can hear the sizzle,
an undercurrent of want.

WHEN NO ONE WILL COME █████████████████████

█████████████ you
forgot, █████████████████
████████████
█████████████████████ your
██████ dreams in with the dust.

Look at yourselves, ███████
███████████████████ weak-kneed
█████████████
in your linen pants, ███████
█ your own shadow, ███████

███████████████████
███ full-sized ████████████
█ old desires
█████████████████████
█████████████████

swerving █████████ all
yearn, ████████████████████
███ wild ██████
█████████████ panting
██████████ in the back seat.

WHEN NO ONE WILL COME TO THE NICKELBACK CONCERT

Don't tell me you
forgot, placed the *photograph*
in the back of the
closet, hid band tees, stuffed your
rockstar dreams in with the dust.

Look at yourselves, adults,
millennials, long grown, weak-kneed
terrified, quaking
in your linen pants, afraid
of your own shadow, long in

the tooth. Does it hurt
to be full-sized and ashamed
of old desires?
Nickelback there *to remind*
you of what you really are:

swerving backroads, all
yearn, hunger, bite and claw, like
the wild *animals*
you used to be, all panting
and fucking in the back seat.

RESURRECTION WITH PUNK ROCK

I shouldn't have listened to
that Billy Talent album.
Ever since, I awoke a ghost.

On the road back from the pool
where I float on my back and let
my brain shut off, I try and conjure
the ghost voice into the air.

My brain, a protection spell
placed, won't do it, refuses to.
Each time I try, I swallow another
rock, but I won't walk out into
the sea with my belly stone-lined.

I can conjure the sounds of all the
others who I ran with, their voices
rough, luminous, a specific vibration,
who are dead or in jail or a million
miles from the person I am now.

Your ghost sits next to me in the
passenger seat, throws back his head
to laugh. It's in this motion that I know
it's still there: your voice, the sounds,
they're too deep in me, like my
autoimmune disorders, inside out.

This is why we don't listen to Billy Talent.
We don't play Nickelback. Metallica

is usually okay, but Avenged Sevenfold,
you can forget it. It's almost October though,
what better time to wake the dead-to-me?

I've told you, I'll say it again, I am
the resurrector. I have many conjuring tools:
a specific album, a Ziploc bag of freckles
collected from light-skinned men, one clear
blue eye, the movie *Tristan and Isolde*,
the book *Here on Earth*, the movie *Spider-Man*,
which we once fucked to against the bathroom
mirror, the film playing in the background,
our eyes latched in the reflection, a never letting go.

I shouldn't wake these ghosts.
I shouldn't yell Billy Talent while
driving 50 in a 35. I am bad-boned,
wrong-footed. I am gluttonous for the pain.

ANOTHER NICKELBACK POEM lol

Nickelback is playing in the summer at the venue we went to and no one will admit that they listened to and liked them, even though they were at the top of the charts on MTV consistently, so i wrote a silly poem about it. i should be grading final papers, but i forgot my rule of no smoking weed before grading, and smoked some of a joint while putting together my Florence & the Machine inspired playlist for 3 hours this morning titled "Girls Against God" lol thus making it a no-grading day & instead a Nickelback poem writing day, which, to me, makes it perfect since it's the spring equinox and all, or Alban Eiler—the light of the day—in Celtic tradition. After all, didn't Nickelback, our lord and teenage savior, provide us with light, longevity, and songs to grieve to, to hang our hands out the window to, to smoke Marlboro Reds under cloudy skies & to fuck by, amen, amen, blessed are those who admit to their own pleasures.

WHEN ████████████████ WE DON'T TALK ABOUT LOVE
████████████████

████████ I ███ loved ████████ I ███ kissed ████████ I learned I
could love ████████████████
████████ while we kissed ████████████████████ long
gone now, ████████████████████████
████████████████████████
████████████████ me on my back████████
████ shhhh, ████████████████ me down a river, ████ I
handed my body over ████████████
yes, you agree ████████████████████████ love this body
until you suffocate it, ████████████████
████████████████████████ let me forget ████
████████████████████████ things I don't say, I
loved to shake ████████████████████████
████████████████ the ████████████████
████ —walls ████████████ the ████ relic of my ████
████████████ busted open ████████████
████████████████████████ gaps ████
████████████████████████████
████████ so much agony ███ this girl in ████ the mirror, ███
████████████ couldn't ████ comprehend.

WHEN WE TALK ABOUT LOVE WE DON'T TALK ABOUT LOVE
—after Raymond Carver and Hanif Abdurraqib

is that before I ever loved a boy, before I ever kissed any, before I learned I could love a girl, or someone who is in-between, before one's hands wrenched my breasts while we kissed on the living room floor of some 4 a.m. long gone now, leaving purple bruises that would fade to putrid yellow, before a boy said *you can't escape me*, before he made sport of breaking my heart, each round him the challenger, me on my back, before he tore it, my heart but also my ~~shhhh~~, piece by piece and drifted me down a river, before I handed my body over like it was a token, a gemstone, a lifetime chip of *yes*, you agree to resolutely and without forgiveness or shame love this body until you suffocate it, before all of that, before the assaults and the pain and the Jesus Christ, if there is even one of you up there, let me forget that boy with the freckled skin, before all that and all the other things I don't say, I loved to shake my hips to *Shakira, Shakira* in front of my mirror for hours and watch the swirl, the groove, the liquid fluid nature of a girl coming into her body—walls behind me painted with the mural relic of my childhood and the brick wall I hand painted, busted open into cloudy blue skies— while wearing those jeans with the leather straps lacing up gaps all down the side of slender ankles, muscled calves, toned thighs, hip flexors that would later cause so much agony that this girl in front of the mirror, long blond hair over gyrating shoulders, couldn't begin to comprehend.

THE ANGEL OF CARRION AND FRUIT FLIES
—after Catherine Broadwall

sits on my shoulder and asks me what I do and don't know.
I don't remember the recipe for biscuits and gravy,

nor do I know how to make the blackberry cheesecake
my mom makes every summer with the juiciest blackberries

pulled from the bramble of her sticker bush. I do remember
that time, months after I left a boy I loved, when he pulled

up in the backseat of a friend's car to the mini-mart, turned
and locked eyes with me in the back of another friend's car.

It had been a year since I started pretending to not love him.
We didn't say a word, didn't nod, didn't blink, until finally

the car I was in began to pull away. I don't know how to
keep the peperomias alive. Or why every sunflower I buy dies,

but the next day when he showed up at my friend's house
and said to me, *I was going to stay away but when you looked*

at me I knew it wasn't over, lives in me like a corpse flower.
Something that used to be natural, magical even, turned the sickening

pink of rotting flesh, feeding off the roots of nearby memories.
Staunch-hearted, root-locked, putrid-sorrow. I don't know how

to weed properly this body garden. When I try to uproot things,
I always break them off right where they go underground.

When they resurface, they multiply like lesions. I don't know
how to stop loving things that hurt me, but I do know about miles:

throw them down, roadblocks, cinder barriers, those green metal signs
with a forged distance, and hope it stops the disease from spreading.

THE YELLOW FLAG
—after Louise Glück

The light, that low blue-hue of March mornings.
I watch the dogs curled on the end of the cushion,
looking out at the start of the world, bushtits
on the mossy limbs of the gum tree, squirrels
performing acrobatics, dangling upside down
from the suet, morsels grasped in tiny palms.

Steam rolls off my *good morning, asshole* mug
and there's dew coating the tall green grass.
Soon the yellow iris will be in bloom, waving
the flag in the blustery storms of April, but
already daffodils swinging bells of spring.

And yet, still I am unsatisfied. This is the cross
I bear: all this blistering beauty, but I want more,
me always sounding like Belle, *Beauty and the
Beast* my soundtrack, arms thrown wide.

More time with the oldest of my dogs, more
early mornings, the velveteen of her neck
crushed over my arms. Less city and more
fields to walk through, more books and more
clean violet air, sharp-toothed after monsooning.

And why shouldn't I? The body's continual
decline in illness. Hunger all that is left. In
the distance a neighbor's house leaches
out puffs of smoke from a chimney I
don't yet have. Two crows circle a
cedarwood round and round and round.

BUCKSHOT BABE

He was elated when he took
me into the woods after a year of
trying to convince me to shoot a gun.
He was adamant I would love it. Insistent.
I held the rifle like he told me, so it wouldn't
kick back and bruise my skin. I shot at the knot on
a tree he motioned to. Hit it. Then, at a small puddle in
the distance, the ripple quaked under the fire. I handed the
gun to him, told him I never wanted to shoot again, walked away.

His face of joy at my clear innate skill fell to disappointment.
Why every boy I loved wanted to pluck the sunflower from
my heart and watch it wilt, I'll never understand. But here
I am, spitting sunflower seeds into a tin can. Ppp-ting,
they ring, like buckshot, they sprout from my fingers,
my toes, like the weed you don't want, they grow
and grow and grow, all testing your patience,
all my body my choice, the buried bodies,
manicured nails, talons, digging up
through the dirt, the sand, the
cement, the bottom of the
sea where you left us.

WHEN ████ A THREAT ████████
████ COMES ████████
May you live ████

You ████ pretend ██ to see ████████

████████ tell yourself ████
████████ an abstraction, ████████ a mirage ████
██ down ████████ black tar ████
██ shimmer of childhood ████ But
that backseat ████████ *threat* ████
████████ that sweet girl in █ your home, ████
████ your eyes ████ the image ████ crouched low

████████ you watch her ████ piece by ██ piece.

████ *encounter* ████████ *fear*
████████

████████ When
████████ her hands ████
████ write █ a poem ████

████ *creature / lonely* ████ *surround us /* ████

████████

████████ yes, ████ yes, ████
██ we won't ████

████████
unsee it, ████████
████████ the truth, ████ how
to be silent, where the ████████ window ██ is █

████████████ to ████████████████████████
██
██████ goodbye ████████████████████.

WHEN THERE'S A THREAT AT MY NIECE'S MIDDLE SCHOOL, SO SHE COMES TO HANG OUT WITH ME FOR THE DAY.

For Mazzy and all the children. May your lives be long.

You can try to pretend not to see them: elementary school, sweet sixteen birthday party, wrong address, flipped a bitch in the wrong driveway, lost on a residential road. You can tell yourself that 163 shootings by the 106th day of the year is an abstraction, some kind of disbelief, a mirage like the ones down the Wyoming highways, black tar in the rearview mirror and the shimmer of childhood behind us. But when the same sister who was in that backseat beside you says *active investigation* & *threat at your 12-year-old niece's middle school*, you take that sweet girl into your home, watch *Peter Rabbit* & *The Lorax*, close your eyes tight to the image of her crouched low under a desk. When she comes in and goes straight to your bigfoot set of poetry magnets on the fridge, you watch her build a world, piece by little piece.

I am alone to encounter a majestic ancient civilization / and some discover fear through the legend of / my escape that only I understand /

and you manage not to put your head in your hands. When a tween who practices active shooter drills, her hands the size of oranges, her smile just as sweet, writes a poem to her fear on the fridge, you write a poem back:

Dark creature / lonely humanoid / they surround us / our people linked / by chase & hunt /

& when she reads the two poems as joined, as a complete landscape, she nods in approval, yes, I agree to this meeting, yes, we are magnet fridge poets and we won't speak of what is happening at your school, at every school, at meetings, at parties, at theaters, at concerts, on a park green. You can try to unsee it, the shadow in the trees, the fury creature hiding from the threat, feigning nonexistence, back turned to the truth, but a child who knows how to be silent, where the blind spots are from a classroom door window, she is in your house, she pats the top of your elder dog's head, just recently diagnosed with a tumor in her abdomen that will end her life in a matter of weeks, and she says goodbye for what may be the last time.

Everywhere I look / bears / bodies blundering wantonly /
through winter / gorged on end-of- year feasts / knowing a change needs
to occur / unable to see / through the blizzard of our collective / traumas / we who climb /
endlessly / to tops of trees / we should be / hunkered / limbs curved around lumbering bear
bodies / heart rates slowed / eight beats per minute / silent night / holy being / instead,
evolution has slipped / past us / salmon downstream / charging us with witness / graying
sky / built up pile of dirty snow near the gutter / huffs and sighs / smoke signals / bear
bodies shivering against harsh wind / or news / other great forces past our control /
sour stomachs and endless / winter stretched out / before us / nests of blankets
makeshift fur / scarves wrapped tight around our throats / bear trap / whipsaw
/ noose / we watch the starlings at the feeder / bickering over bricks of
seed / each claw and growl / grumble of hunger / buried deep under
ice we cannot / thaw / we try not to weep / when the
golden hour comes / seen by our ungodly eyes /

PARTNER

I tried to make this home a house but his patience never ran thin and we got a second dog and their clacking nails filled up the halls and their fur clumped on couches and in corners and books stacked slowly, building skyscrapers and satellites against the walls, and dishes piled in sinks, on tables, and unkempt on the stove while laundry spun round and round and rain tinkled down on the roof and neighbors heard my moods and music and foul tongue, and the crows watched me pace and beat the four walls of brilliance and years of kindness and laughter filled up the firepit and wrought kindling from my loins and love wasn't proclaimed it was a foundation we didn't mean to lay down for.

AT THE FROG PARK

What we love we must consume wholly.

—Kelly Webster, *We Are Changed to Deer at the Broken Places*

Frogs the size of dimes
scatter as we near the shore
of Frog Lake, light and
dark brown bodies hold vital
organs in a hollow space.

Frogs like stones, like mud
until they reach the water
and kick gracefully
away, like my body held
under the blue at the pool.

My niece darts out quick,
frog-tongued to capture her prey.
In her preteen hands,
small web of toes spread before
launching into the unknown.

At the frog park as
children, my sister and I
would slide our fragile
lean bodies down the mouth of
a large frog, our mother, pool-

side, waiting for the
splash at the other end. At
Frog Lake, we find one
lone emerald body, I scoop
it and place it *gentle, gently*

now, I say, hand pressed
to my niece's, and watch the
catapult. She walks,
ankles deep in the sinking,
mud slurping our feet with each

step, making our way
down shore, our eyes peeled for more
leaping bodies, an
abstraction of light. I tell her
she's too deep in the water

for the tiny life
in her hands, but she doesn't
release. Suddenly,
we see the dart as he thrusts
from her hands, falls into deep

water, alabaster
belly to the sky, body
still and we scramble
to lift it from the depths of
shallows, unfathomable,

resurrect it from
almost death, place it ashore.
I worry for her then,
not the frog, my niece, already
holding too tight, things she loves.

WHEN ▮▮▮▮▮▮ DYING

1.

She is flopping ▮▮▮▮▮▮▮▮
She is releasing ▮▮▮▮
She is stepping up ▮▮▮▮▮▮▮▮▮▮▮▮
▮▮▮▮▮▮▮▮▮▮▮▮
She is digging ▮▮▮▮▮▮▮▮▮▮
▮▮▮▮▮▮▮▮▮▮▮▮▮▮▮▮ she is flailing
▮▮▮▮▮▮▮▮
She is watching ▮▮▮▮▮▮▮▮▮▮.

She's ▮▮▮▮▮▮▮▮▮▮▮▮▮▮▮▮▮▮
▮▮▮▮▮▮▮▮▮▮▮▮▮▮▮▮▮▮▮▮
▮▮▮▮▮▮▮▮▮▮▮▮ ultimately our
decision ▮▮▮▮▮▮▮▮?

▮▮ she is ▮ *harrumphing.*
She is snorting.
She is barking ▮▮▮▮▮▮▮▮.
She is pacing ▮▮▮▮ at all hours ▮▮▮.

She is holding secrets in ▮▮▮▮▮▮▮▮▮▮
▮▮▮▮▮▮ the back of her throat ▮▮▮▮▮▮▮▮
▮▮▮▮▮▮▮▮▮▮▮▮▮▮▮▮▮▮
▮▮▮▮▮▮▮▮.

▮▮▮▮▮▮▮▮▮▮▮▮▮▮ the ones about the
end ▮▮▮▮▮▮▮▮▮▮▮▮▮▮ of
the light streaming ▮▮▮▮▮▮▮▮
▮▮▮▮▮▮▮▮▮▮▮▮▮▮
▮▮▮▮▮▮▮▮

dying is also

a little half prance,

up in the air

daintily through April's rain-drenched grass.

bridging the distance between

here, now,

2.

It is fuchsia, marigolds,
snapdragons, dahlias, pansies, thyme, the delicate
touching

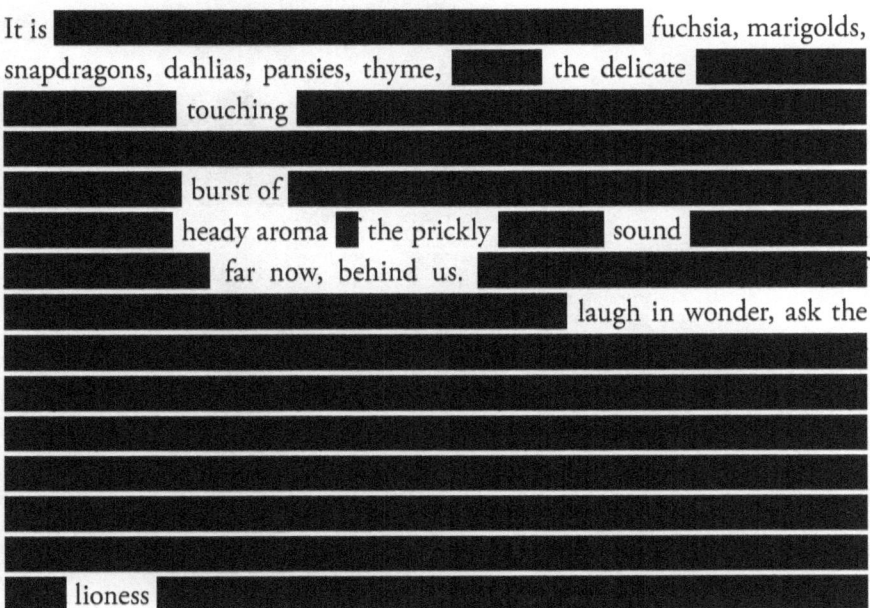

burst of
heady aroma the prickly sound
far now, behind us.
laugh in wonder, ask the

lioness

when she is ready to ███████████ go to the ███

blinding buttercup yellow,
end. Carefully,

begin the
march, turn
up up up, traverse the gap between

the end, shake out the
disappearing act, its own sort of magic.
their little bodies , their
tiny legs, their tummies, unmoving.

3.

She in the soil
glorious, stupendous

Relief.

4.

███████████████████████████████████
███████████████████████████████████
███████████████████████████████████
███████████████████████████████████
███████████████████████████████████
███████████████████████████████████
███████████████████████████████████

I wake up and she is running ████████████
█████████████ wild ██████████ living ███

dying under the cherry blossom tree. I want ████

███████████████████████████████████
███████████████████████████████████
█████████ my dog ██████████████████
███████████████ I want my dog ████
███████ I ██ want █████████████████
██████ my dog ██████████████████████
███████████████████████████████████

██████████ here in this bed, curled around one another,
███████████████ one arm curled under the weight
of one velveteen neck, ███████████████████

███████████████████████████████████
███████████████████████████████████
███████████████████████████████████
████████████ I am only ██████████ One
long, lone, howl.

5.

She

rest her head

I watch   I watch

I watch

I   carry

her.

I dig a hole in the damp soil.

I

sniff the air,

Snout raised. I

Move slowly.

her

I see

her.

over us. I witness.

WHEN MY DOG IS DYING

1.

She is flopping down on the couch.

She is releasing a big sigh.

She is stepping up on my chest and licking and licking and licking

my face and neck for as long as I will allow it.

She is digging at the blanket until we cover her up,

making sure to leave her nose uncovered, and when we don't, she is flailing

her head til we fix our mistake.

She is watching the squirrels and crows at the birdfeeder.

She's sometimes bleeding from a tumor in her abdomen and then laying on the same spot on the floor for hours, not eating and scaring us into taking her to the ER, making us debate putting her down, like it's ultimately our decision to make, which it is, but also, is it?

But she is also *harrumphing*.

She is snorting.

She is barking at the kids at the little free library.

She is pacing around the house at all hours of the night.

She is holding secrets in her mouth which is what we call when we shove the pills all the way to the back of her throat and she fakes giving us kisses but later somehow spits the pills out onto the couch, on the rug, in to her bedtime water bowl we keep in the bedroom.

But also, she is holding secrets, many secrets, especially the ones about the end and when it's good for her, when it's the right time, when she's tired of the light streaming through the window on to her face and listening to the rain fall and the windows being open, tired of her snout raised to the air and sniffing for scents we cannot and do not smell.

My dog is dying but she is also staring across the room at me.

She is doing a little half prance, what her arthritis will allow,

picking a toy off the ground and tossing it up in the air and trying

to catch it before decimating it with the power of her now busted teeth.

She is the little spoon, my body curled tightly around it.

She licks and licks and licks my partners face when he lies down

next to her on her dog bed and cries and cries and cries.

She is stepping daintily through April's rain-drenched grass.

She is breathing.

She is bridging the distance between

the couch and the coffee table,

nosing at an empty bowl, her distended belly

hanging low under the weight of her collapsing back.

She is here, now, still beside me.

2.

It is spring. At the store, filling my cart to the brim with fuchsia, marigolds, snapdragons, dahlias, pansies, thyme, rubbing the delicate leaves between my fingers and touching them to my nostrils, a tomato plant even though I can't eat tomatoes, haven't been able to for years and years and years, but I remember the burst of tomato plants lining my grandparents backyard in California, the heady aroma of the prickly stalk, the sound of my grandma Janice's laugh, so far now, behind us. At the checkout, a sign: Bag of Ladybugs, Nature's Natural Pest Control! And I laugh in wonder, ask the attendant if this is real. His face blank as he points toward a hook where they hang. Inside the mesh bag, they press up against each other, their little legs pedaling. At home, my dogs muscles wasting, her skeleton more apparent in her shoulders where the bone presses out, the dip behind it, the thinness of her butt that I boost, repeatedly, onto the couch, the bed, the outdoor benches, the picnic table, first to the seat, then to the top, where she lounges like a lioness and then throws her head back and barks and barks and barks when she is ready to get hoisted down. At home, I go to the iris's where the caterpillars have been feasting, pocked holes aligning each stem, leaf, spathe, not yet burst open, not yet blinding buttercup yellow, like we all won't die in the end. Carefully, I cut the mesh bag so as not to hurt one single ladybird, tug at the opening and there they are, hundreds of them, they begin their march, I turn my arm and a dozen of them, their little red bodies, their little speckled backs, march up up up, traverse the gap between my arm and the rolled up sleeve of my button up, one alights in my hair, dangles blissfully from a blond thread, meanwhile, they cover the leaves, the stems, marching out, some bodies on top of bodies doing spring deeds in the 80 degree air, others test out their wings, open, close, open, fly off, land on my face, my arms, my legs, the continual march. I carry them from flower to herb to flower to yard, they zip around. At the end, I shake out the rest, hundreds already gone, off into the air, a disappearing act, its own sort of magic. At the end of the bag, casualties, their hard little bodies drop to the soil, their tiny legs, curled in tightly to their tummies, unmoving. My dog stares out the open screen window.

3.

Pig-eared, pot-bellied.

My face, snout-coated, kiss-crusted.

She is prancing, she bunny-hops toward

The maple tree. She digs in the soil and comes up,

Dirt-eater, mineral-muncher, gloriously, stupendously

Alive. "I hope your dog . . ." my students trail off, unsure

Of their condolences, how to end. "Lives forever?"

I suggest to their sheer, utter, dumbfounded

Relief.

4.

I write a poem about my dog aging. I write a poem about her slowing down, slower still. I write a poem where my dog kills a rat. I write a poem about how one dog almost killed a crow and how the other dog was ushered back inside by my hands while my partners hands saved the crow. I dream about cancer and tumors. I dream about them finding tumors in my body, in my dogs' body, again, in my body. We are tumor lined. I wake up and she is running in her sleep at the bottom of the bed. I think how wild it is, that there we are, living right up until our death. I think about writing a poem about her dying under the cherry blossom tree. I want the day we put her down to be sunny and for her to go to sleep quietly under the cherry blossom, *Kanzan Sakura*, and while she falls to sleep, while we cry over her body, petals will fall down as the wind lightly blows. I want my dog dying poem to last forever. Part 2, part 3, part 5 thousand and 33. I want my dog dying poem to live forever. I don't want to write an end to it. I write a poem where my dog doesn't die, where I don't die, nobody dies, you get another life, you get another life, we are all going to live forever, here in this bed, curled around one another, one dog paw on my back, one arm curled under the weight of one velveteen neck, she pushes her head up and back, the better to lick my face, while behind me, another dog who will never die, snores loudly, mouth open, teefs showing. I only write poems for my dogs now, sorry for those of you who came expecting my usual. I am only a dog poem now. One long, lone, howl.

5.

For an hour, maybe more,

I lay down beside my dog

under the maple tree. Little

bursts of green drift over us.

She shreds a bright pink

tennis ball, sometimes stopping

to rest her head on it like a

pillow. I watch her. I watch

the sky. I watch the swallows
swoop around cedarwoods.
I watch a group of ants carry
a fallen soldier. I watch her.
I dig a hole in the damp soil.
I don't worry about my damp
butt or grass rashes or bugs
in my hair. She sniffs the air,
snout raised. I watch a slug
move slowly. Save it when the
ants pile on. There are little pink
tufts of tennis ball fur in her
mouth. I pull them out and
toss them to the wind. I see
a tiny centipede, a green beetle,
a black one, a bee buzzing.
I watch her. The wind blows
lightly over us. I witness.

AFTER SHE TAKES HER LAST BREATH

I curl around her loose form—
how empty a body
seems, but I swear

she's still there
all that love tucked away
at the seams.

When they carry
her body to the opened
back of the maroon

SUV in our driveway,
I go behind them,
gathering her things.

I toss things, getting
rid of evidence of her,
like a seismic gap can be resealed.

Her giant rubber dog bowl
called the horsey troth because
I didn't know its size when I ordered it.

Shreds of torn up dog toys,
the dog bed she started to die on
where she lifted her snout, placed

it first, on my mouth,
held, held, still holding.
Then, to my eye, pressing it closed.

Then the dog bed I carried
outside, where my partner laid
down her body for the last time.

But there are things I keep.
Her pink collar and pink rain jacket.
The sound of her bark and the weight

of her tiny paw in the palm of my hand.

LOW PLACES

At the river we walk
up the bank to the trails
& back down to the water.
My niece leading the charge.
The third time she does this,
I stay above & she waves her hand,
beckoning me to come back down.
She picks up a sand cricket
by its legs, brushes it off until
we can both see its coloring is
made to look like sand, camouflage
marvel. When a small rabbit isn't
scared of us, lets us get too close,
I say, *that isn't good, it's lost its fear
of humans*, so she chases it away. All
afternoon we plod, my friend grief
around this stretch of woods &
she doesn't say a word about it.
She only points & says *look, look*,
drags a stick through the water, pulls
out a discarded crawdad shell,
rattles off facts to me about birds
& other strange & mysterious things.

DIRT EATERS

Nobody came to clean my house when she died.
No one to dust away her dander, her sound echoing
through the hallways, the spot on the couch where
she'd sleep and chase wild things in her dreams.

My mom brought me a neon orange pot of geraniums,
to chase away the darkness, I suppose. While my
mother-in-law, if there was a name for the mother
of your partner of a decade who you aren't married to,
brought a pot of tomatoes, though I didn't know what
they were until late summer, and now I watch them slowly ripen
from pale green to cherry red. While all around them the grass
where she released her last gasping breath curdles in the hottest
summer on earth. Tomatoes are their own kind of acceptance,
I guess, the way they fall into your hands, ripe off the vine.

Nobody could bring her back. That's the truth of the matter.
I am the resurrector, the dreamscaper, the small
and insignificant God. I conjure her into the night,
the same way I resurrect all past loves. What does the moon
know anyway, all lofty heights? Here in the dirt we are
devastated, we are digging with our teeth searching for
nutrients or sanity or something to sustain us. People move on,
or so I'm told, but these well-worn spots on the rug
where I drag out the bodies, parade them through the hall
night after night while my partner sleeps, tells a different
story. And who is coming to clean up the soil I track in my wake?

WHEN ▮ KATYDIDS ▮ SING ▮
▮

Mostly, I'll ▮ warble ▮,
katydids playing ▮, how wind
▮ sounds like ▮
▮ mouths parting.

▮ my desires ▮ exist.

When ▮
▮ our throats ▮
▮ scorch
▮ under ▮ the waves swallow
▮, starve us, the ▮
drop dead, ▮ curl ▮ your love ▮
extinction, your love ▮

You ▮

▮
▮ deny ▮ what is ▮
▮ against one another,
▮ the kingfisher ▮ the river,
▮ your name ▮ .

WHEN THE KATYDIDS STOP SINGING

—after Claire Wahmanholm

Mostly, I'll miss the sounds: warblers warbling,
katydids playing the symphony, how wind blowing
through forest sounds like a rushing river or waterfall
nearby, my niece's laughter, the memory of mouths parting.

I can't shrink my desires by pretending they don't exist.

When the world ends, when we choke on the remnants
of the burning wood, the ash thick in our throats like
sarcophagus dust, like mummification, when we scorch
to death under an unrelenting sun, when the waves swallow
us, the ice all gone, starves us, the bees line the asphalt,
drop dead, even you will curl, crust up, your love a mass
extinction, your love an avocado seed, no water left to plant it.

You, who take for granted all that you see before you.

Only I feel the small feet of the dragonfly on my leg
without brushing it away, denying what is sacred, watch
the katydid draw its strings gracefully against one another,
point to the kingfisher that follows us as we float down the river,
preserve your name, ice-crusted, shell-shocked.

WHAT IS HOLY

Early September, one lone goose,
first of the season, calls above in the sky.
I don't pretend to know what the world
has in store for us, what waits after, or why
one dog, a few weeks after the other passes,
begins having seizures. Nothing makes sense
and what I believe is holy doesn't match
with what the fascists say.

But here, this lone goose, one lone honk,
here this quiet chill in the air, the frogs croaking
at night as we fall asleep, the weight of a dog paw,
its prints in the mud, in its sleep running.

I am what is holy, sings the frog.
I am what is holy, cries the goose.
I am what is holy, howls the dog.
And the mud squelches under foot,
and the pattern of the moss on the tree,
and the vibration of a heart beating wildly
that strange staccato of fear and love.

IN WHICH SHE SUFFERS A HAUNTING—

—just because her ghosts release
on the world a thousand banshees
doesn't mean she's released

from pain—pain being oldest
of languages, foul-mouthed,
long-toothed, triumphant
in its ever-changing nature, ever-
staying the same—maybe that's why

the woman took the carving
spoon to her eye, scooped it out like
it was meant for some child's
ice cream cone: one scoop or two?
Dripping maraschino cherry red, syrup
pooling on lips: you can release

a thousand haunts on the world,
never enough, not now, not
when you peer, pull back the curtain, look into
dark cavern where there used to be

glassy eye—you see the ghosts, sardines in a can, mouths
agape—the pressure that must have caused: inhumane,
inhuman, the suffering;
but you watch her reach

to stony ground, pack eye socket
tight with cool comfort of river
rocks; she begins swallowing

—sandstone, basalt, siltstone—rocking
them in there, as it were, all the little
haunts, sealing   the   gaps.

JANUARY TIDES

Each morning I make a cup of tea,
my hands wrapped tightly around.

These are the things that make up a life.

Some mornings, I don't drink the tea,
only let it hold me the way all water does.

This morning I smelled spring,
my window cracked & green moss looking in.

Now it's misting, one of those January fugue
states & the branches bare arthritic lady fingers.

I don't collect the rain water in jars or any
water for that matter, but I think about doing it.

Isn't that the same thing?

We drive to the river at dusk. She parks
her car and we sit there talking until the horizon

meets the water and we can't tell the two apart.
She doesn't want to walk down to the bank.

I am disappointed but I don't say. I just watch
the darkness fall & imagine my body submerged.

WHEN LIVING ▇

All night ▇ another woman. Repeatedly, ▇ her body ▇

▇ she tells ▇

▇ something ▇

validating ▇

everything ▇, wrestling ▇ shut, ▇

all my ▇ wants. ▇ a woman ▇

▇ disappointed with the second half of ▇

life. ▇

▇ raise the body ▇ the dream ▇ body,

▇ wake ▇ sigh, lips

▇ cold ▇ open ▇ me.

WHEN LIVING IN DREAMS

All night I dream of sex with another woman. Repeatedly, I pull her body to mine. This isn't scarcity but its opposite. My therapist has me fill out a PTSD questionnaire. When we meet, she tells me I scored high on all the markers, giving me the formal diagnosis for something I already knew. This is both validating and plaguing. I thought I had been doing a very good job of placing everything in cardboard boxes, wrestling the folds shut, writing across them with sharpie: abuse, assault, medical trauma, heart-stopping, chronic illness, all my little wants. In a review for my memoir, a woman writes how she was disappointed with the second half of my book, how it became all about dreams, when what she wanted was to know more about what was going on in the writer's life. *My life.* All day I stew on this. What you don't understand, I want to write to her, is that sometimes the only place where I am living is in dreams. I raise the body of the dream woman above my body, place my mouth where I dare not speak. I wake into a sigh, lips parted, the darkness of 5 a.m. and the cold September air seeping through the open window surrounds me.

WHILE SLEEPING

I miss so many things: the possibility of northern lights, shooting stars, lunar eclipses. I miss the hunter moon, strawberry, corn, full sturgeon, milk moon. But also, I meet some of you there, especially the ones that are dead, like my dog, two months gone now. I cry while I hold her in my arms. I walk the streets with an overdosed best friend, her hair still pale yellow the way of the young and blond, not yet aged and darkened by life. I go swimming with my middle school boyfriend and childhood friend, here his body no longer ravaged by cancer, his beard grown in full. Here I make love often to old lovers and new. Kiss boys I used to love, kiss girls I could have. I often miss dusk even, already tucked into bed with a book, and I miss the sounds of the frogs nearby, their croaking, the crickets, their chirping. I miss driving around in the dark of looping backroads, the fog creeping around the bends, and I miss the silence, that sweet tang.

ILLNESS: JUST A PLACE WHERE I KEEP MY BONES

I have risen twig,
starling, blunder.

When all you want
is above or below you

and you plead with a god
you've never believed in:

Sever your hands.
Sever your hands I implore you.

And the great battle with the body
is never won.

Fall back. Fall back, now.
Let the red clay dust consume you.

THEY CALL IT GETTING CLEAN, SO WHY ARE MY NAILS STILL DIRT-CRUSTED?

On the side of the street
a man with his pants down
around his ankles, body
flailing—up, down, up, down,
up, down, arms in the wind,
arms held tightly to the body,
up, down, face contorted—

on the corner outside the 7-Eleven
a huddle, masses of bodies,
they tear from the pipe tilted
upside down—the same way
you used to hit the weed pipe,
back when I didn't know better,
didn't know the turning meant
your experiences meth-lined,
heroine-hearted—broad daylight
and nowhere to go, no peace to make
with a world that doesn't want them,
the woman who turns her face as she drives by.

On Sandy Boulevard a woman stands
on the sidewalk facing the cars, naked
from the belly button down, eyes made of
glass, each one an ocean away from here;
the woman walking the same stretch of street,
her face gone hollow, all bones and shards and
bone shards. Each one a backstory similar to my own.

On this street, this time a huddle
outside the plaid pantry, boys I could

have known, you could be there, you
could be strung out under the wildfire sky,
drought-tongued, skylight ceiling
overhead, you could be the next article
I pull up, the next GoFundMe for the loss
of a loved one who struggled with addiction.
One day I'll be standing over your grave,
like you stood over mine.
I'll be the one holding the matches

WHEN YOU ▮▮▮ STALK ▮ THE ▮▮ STREETS

You and I ▮▮▮

▮▮▮ quiver in our ▮▮ deer-fear. Your hands ▮▮▮ your tongue, ▮▮▮ your ▮▮▮ skin-salted. We ▮▮▮

▮▮ bruised ▮▮▮

▮▮▮ sprawled ▮▮

▮▮ split ▮▮▮

▮▮ swallowing ▮▮▮ the river mud ▮▮. Smoked ▮▮▮ rolled ▮▮▮ held ▮▮▮ licked ▮▮▮ We ▮▮ pretend that ▮▮▮ love ▮▮▮ would ▮▮ ▮▮▮ end, ▮▮ banish ▮▮▮ our names ▮▮▮.

WHEN YOUR SILHOUETTE STALKS THE CITY STREETS

But you wouldn't be here anyway. You and I, we aren't city-lined, concrete-hearted. Our backdrop was always Douglas fir, sap-scented, arteries river-lined, sand-crusted eyelids, the quiver in our chests, deer-fear. Your hands unfurled on my skin like fern fronds, your tongue, the under belly, your taste Marlboro-soaked, skin-salted. We were at the mouth where the ocean meets the sea, and we were the mouth, cussing and fighting and kissing until we were bruised at the hip. We fucked in the soil and pretended our hearts weren't on the line, weren't one downed-tree, tires screeching, sprawled across logging roads split wide open. We jumped off piers into the crashing sound of waves, swallowing the hurt in us, let the river mud suck to our feet. Smoked where we could, curtain of woods in the background when you rolled the dollar bill, held it out to me, licked-powder from your booze-soaked kisses. We played pretend: that you didn't love me / that I would die for you. Both liars in the end, both banished, tree people sent, one to the city and one to the desert where only the crows and the ravens dare to speak our names in unison.

I COULD BECOME SOMEONE ELSE

I could make a home
anywhere   crawl inside
     cedarwood misting in crows

not make home   be home

transplant wants

step into leafless tree bones
fall down a barrel of snapdragon trumpets
     taste endless spring

call up my ghosts
     wherever.

SORRY YOU DON'T BURN WITH YEARNING

1. In a workshop I ask the writers to compile a list of longings based off fragments from the essay, "The End of Longing" by Chelsea Hodson.

2. It's been storming, volcanic blustering gusts. When I walk the remaining dog, there are tree limbs scattered all over the ground and leaves lift around our feet. I look up into the shake and shimmy of the branches, willing another branch to fall.

3. On the list we include: longing for love in all the wrong places / the illusion of love.

4. At the beach before the rain wall moves in, we let our dog off leash, people so far ahead and behind that we fake safety for a few minutes of letting us all run free, pretend the shackles aren't there, disappear the endless nights when we wake to his body rigid, convulsing there on the comforter between us, my partner holding and me injecting, his mouth roiling over, a sea of foam. Here, we release the hounds in us, the hound with us, a small shell of forgetting. We prod the jellyfish with our toes as we walk by. We absorb the punches.

5. After our free-write time, a workshop attendee says, *I didn't write, there was nothing in this prompt on longing for me.* And how sad that must be, how small, all that unused shriveled up, dumped in the compost desire. I think it's inside her. I think it's gnashing its teeth.

6. On the longing list we include: longing for the past / for the things we know we will lose / for the things that we don't have yet or never will.

7. Hodson writes, "What's the point of longing? To continue."

8. I dream I meet an old love out by the river. He's standing on the banks with a fishing rod. I am on the shore, flopping in my new fish skin, trying to breathe. He picks me up, splits me jaw bone to tail, slides a key between ribs, then throws me back in. Down here, under the silt, a fractured breath.

9. My little brother calls, he says it's bad news, *who died*, I say, my stomach muscles clenched tight, waiting for the scalpel, it's going to cut me clavicle to sternum, pull down the sheaths of my chest, find the place where the first knife went in. The coroner will point to it and say, cause of death: hemorrhagic fever /contact with an infected animal / your lips still there under the bone. When my brother says a name that isn't yours, I seal the wounds back up, stitch by stitch. We don't have to open you yet.

10. In a message from a friend she says, *your book is a gateway drug to yearning.*

11. I ask my partner if he is going to come to my poetry reading this weekend. I never pressure him, because him coming also limits what I'm comfortable reading. I want to be unapologetic up there at the mic. *I don't think I want to cry about our dead dog*, he says.

12. I make my own list of longings: to be another person, to live another life, to be who I used to be, to fuck in the back seat of a car, to run, to swim, to fight, to bleed, to stick my arms out and spin and spin and spin, to eat all the foods I no longer can, to kiss, to be down on my knees in the mud snout pressed to earth snuffling for the scent of roots, to kiss more, to walk down a dark street holding hands with a stranger, to resurrect my dead, to lie, to cover myself in leaves, to sing, to jump off a cliff into the rush of water, to fill my ears with it, to drown out the sound, only the waves crashing over me, to drown out your name, to capture a bird, to be a bird, to stop remembering your body above my body—your hands on my ankles, thighs, hips, torso, chest, neck, lips—to heal, to pluck out the moon, to pluck out your eyes, to swallow them whole.

ACKNOWLEDGMENTS & NOTES

Thank you to the editors and readers of these journals and presses where these poems first appeared, sometimes in earlier versions or with different titles:

Cosmic Daffodil: "The Yellow Flag"
Cream Scene Carnival Magazine: "Resurrection with Punk Rock" and "In Which She Suffers a Haunting"
Lit Shark: "When the Katydids Stop Singing," "When ██ Katydids ██ Sing██" and "At the Frog Park"
Pile Press: "Triptych from a Box of Darkness," "When We Don't Talk About Love When We Talk About Love," and "When No One Will Come to the Nickelback Concert"

"The Yellow Flag," "When We First Learn She's Dying," "When My Dog is Dying," "After She Takes Her Last Breath," "While Sleeping," and "Dirt Eaters" appeared in *Dirt Eaters*, my chapbook out from Bottlecap Press.

"Triptych from a Box of Darkness" starts with "Someone I once loved" which is a slightly altered borrowing from "The Uses of Sorrow" by Mary Oliver.

THANKS

First and foremost, thanks to the universe and Andy for bringing me the pig, Roxy, my sweet pit bull, into my life. It has been the highlight of my life to love her and witness her and watch her flame out like the brilliant little star she was. Thanks to Catherine Broadwall, so often the first reader of any of my poems and to Kelly Gray, whose workshops give me a space to mine my darkness. Thanks to Courtney LeBlanc, for giving *Little Deaths* a home and seeing in it what I hoped would be seen. Thanks to Jennifer Militello, Allison Titus, and Melissa Crowe, for taking the time to read advanced versions of this and blurb it. Thanks to my support network which consists of, but is not limited to: my parents and siblings, my partner, my dogs (yes, I am still saying dogs, though by the time this book comes out it will have been over a year), my first responders—Jordana, Brittany, Paula, Ani, Andrea, and Delilah—who were all there most when I needed them. Thanks to Emily Perkovich, who gave me my first real shot in this publishing world and who continues to be a great creative partner and a guiding hand in a dark world. Mostly, thanks to the women, you all are miracles, you all amaze me with your brilliance and your kindness and your heart. And thanks, of course, to every good dog out there, for making our lives immeasurably better than they would be without you.

ABOUT THE AUTHOR

Shilo Niziolek has written *Fever, atrophy,* and *Pigeon House* (Querencia Press), *A Thousand Winters In Me* (Gasher Press), *I Am Not an Erosion: Poems Against Decay* (Ghost City Press), and *Dirt Eaters* (Bottlecap Press). Her work has appeared in *Juked, Honey Literary, West Trade Review, Entropy, Pork Belly Press,* and *Phoebe Journal,* among others. Shilo is a writing instructor at Clackamas Community College, a workshop facilitator for the Literary Arts, and is the editor and co-founder of the literary magazine, *Scavengers.* Find her on Instagram @shiloniziolek

ABOUT THE PRESS

Riot in Your Throat is an independent press that
publishes fierce, feminist poetry.

Support independent authors, artists, and presses.

Visit us online:
www.riotinyourthroat.com

RIOT IN YOUR THROAT BOOKS

Sarah Beddow   *Dispatches from Frontier Schools*
Kathryn Bratt-Pfotenhauer   *Bad Animal*
Kimberly Casey   *Where the Water Begins*
Sonia Greenfield   *All Possible Histories*
Brett Elizabeth Jenkins   *Brilliant Little Body*
Melissa Fite Johnson   *Green*
Melissa Fite Johnson   *Midlife Abecedarian*
Courtney LeBlanc   *Exquisite Bloody, Beating Heart*
Shilo Niziolek   *Little Deaths*
Laura Passin   *Borrowing Your Body*
Sara Quinn Rivara   *Little Beast*
Laurie Rachkus Uttich   *Somewhere, a Woman
   Lowers the Hem of Her Skirt*
Karen J Weyant   *Avoiding the Rapture*

www.ingramcontent.com/pod-product-compliance
Lightning Source LLC
Chambersburg PA
CBHW030501130626
46549CB00007B/2818